Steel Rails On The Old Trails In The Western Pacific Country

Charles Carroll Goodwin

In the interest of creating a more extensive selection of rare historical book reprints, we have chosen to reproduce this title even though it may possibly have occasional imperfections such as missing and blurred pages, missing text, poor pictures, markings, dark backgrounds and other reproduction issues beyond our control. Because this work is culturally important, we have made it available as a part of our commitment to protecting, preserving and promoting the world's literature. Thank you for your understanding.

STEEL RAILS ON THE OLD TRAILS
IN THE WESTERN PACIFIC COUNTRY

BY
C. C. GOODWIN OF SALT LAKE CITY

ISSUED BY
THE PASSENGER DEPARTMENT OF
THE WESTERN PACIFIC
RAILWAY

E. L. LOMAX
PASSENGER TRAFFIC MANAGER

STEEL RAILS ON THE OLD TRAILS
IN THE WESTERN PACIFIC COUNTRY

PASSENGERS on the Western Pacific Railway, I would have a confidential talk with you, an old-time garrulous talk such as was common around the camp fires of the West, before the inconveniences of living in houses became a fixed habit.

A Plain Talk

I heard one of you complaining of the long, weary railroad ride. Did that gentleman understand that he was riding through the deserts and mountains on a one per cent maximum grade, which seems easy enough to the passenger in the Pullman, but which in truth represents one of the greatest engineering feats of the marvelous twentieth century? On this road from Salt Lake City to San Francisco, for nearly seven hundred miles, the grade is less than one-half of one per cent, and to secure a one per cent grade down the canyon of Feather River meant the very highest order of engineering skill and an appalling outlay of millions of dollars. Nothing like it in the Sierras was ever before attempted, nothing like it will ever be. What tires the passenger is the monotony of riding on an almost level roadbed.

Traveling on a One Per Cent Maximum Grade

But there is more to this route. It follows one of the principal trails of the Argonauts of " '49" and was

The Way of the Argonauts

in the long ago consecrated by their struggles and their toil to subdue the savagery of the land and make it possible for civilization on unsoiled sandals to follow.

Let me tell you about those old trails.

The Last Resting Place of Many

Up to the coming of the railroad this trail was lined with skeletons of dead animals, the wrecks of wagons, and not infrequently, a little to one side of the trail, could be seen a mound which marked the spot where had been hastily buried some emigrant, who, overwearied, had fallen asleep. Life is filled with sorrows and tragedies; the overland trails had their full quota of both.

A Greek March

The account of the retreat of the ten thousand under Xenophon has thrilled the world for three-and-twenty centuries. The Greek leader tells how that retreat was "conducted over rapid rivers, through vast deserts and over mountain tops to the sea." The route (1,135 leagues) was just about as long as is the distance from Chicago or St. Louis to the mouth of the Willamette. But Xenophon's band was made up of veteran soldiers, made hard as iron by many campaigns.

The Several Trails

There were several trails spreading out from about the present site of Granger, Wyoming, and a glance at the map will show the various routes from Granger to northern Oregon and California. One trail followed, from Granger, what is now the route of the Oregon Short Line, via Soda Springs to Fort Hall (which is now Pocatello, Idaho), then along the foothills and in sight of Snake River to the Blue Mountains and over them to the valley of the Columbia River, Portland and Astoria.

The First Trail

The Second Trail

One trail, after the exodus to California set in, was followed by many from Fort Hall, westerly to about where Alturas, in northern California, now is,

IN THE WESTERN PACIFIC COUNTRY

and thence down the Pitt River to the Sacramento Valley.

The Third Trail — One trail followed from Granger into Salt Lake Valley and, passing to the south of Great Salt Lake, wended its way via Deep Creek and Ruby Valley on over the Nevada ranges, crossing the Toyabe Range north of what is now Austin, Nevada, to the sink of the Carson and up the Carson to where Genoa now is and thence over the Sierras via the Hangtown trail to Placerville. This route was later taken by the Pony Express and overland stages.

The Fourth Trail — One trail followed almost to Deep Creek, then turned northwest and intercepted the main emigrant trail at a point about where Wells, Nevada, now is.

The Fifth Trail — One trail followed from the Salt Lake Valley, went north of Salt Lake, then crossed over the desert to the west to the headwaters of the Humboldt, through Winnemucca, and down the Humboldt to the sink (Humboldt Lake), then crossed over the divide to the Truckee River, up the Truckee to where the town of Truckee now is, then skirted Donner Lake and pursued its way over the Donner Lake Pass and came out about where Dutch Flat, California, now stands.

The Sixth Trail — One trail kept on due west from about where Winnemucca, Nevada, now is, crossing the desert north of Pyramid Lake and finding a pass some twelve miles north of Beckwith Pass into Long Valley, either turned south up Long Valley to Beckwith Pass and thence through that pass, or turned north down the valley to Honey Lake and thence over the Sierras via the Lassen or Fremont Pass, coming out about where Red Bluff now is.

The Seventh Trail — One trail turned to the northwest from where Winnemucca now is, and, crossing the Black Rock Desert and passing north of Honey Lake, likewise took the Lassen or Fremont Pass over the Sierras. Others turned north and west from where Reno now is, and over a low divide reached Long Valley, followed down that valley to Beckwith Pass, thence via Sierra and Mohawk valleys to Quincy in American Valley, or, turning north through a low divide in the hills north of Sierra Valley, passed on through Clover and Genesee valleys to Indian Valley and thence on to Quincy.

The Way of the Argonauts Over Rivers, Deserts and Mountains

Thus you will see that the great bulk of the people who first peopled California went over these various routes—a long, heroic march.

But along the overland trails were rivers and deserts and mountain tops to cross, with savage tribes on either hand, and this was essayed by delicate women and little children, though the whole route was flanked by hardship and sickness and want and savage tribes.

The Western Pacific Line Traverses this land of Romance

It will be seen from the map that the Western Pacific starts out of Salt Lake City on the old Pony Express and overland stage trail, then diverges to the northwest until it strikes the main emigrant trail and follows it to Winnemucca, then where the old trail bends to the southwest it keeps straight along the less frequented trail and, running as nearly west as possible to insure least grades, finds its way to the old Beckwith Pass and thence on through Sierra and Mohawk valleys, continues to American Valley and thence down the North Fork of the Feather River until it debouches into the Sacramento Valley at Oroville.

Beckwith Pass

The advantages of this route have been known from the first. Beckwith Pass is merely the breaking down of Sierra Valley into Long Valley. Thousands of people drove their tired wagons through this pass and later trotted their buggies through it, and would never have known that it was the eastern pass through the Sierras had they not been told that it was.

A Report to the "Big Four"

The first chief engineer of the old Central Pacific Railroad, Theodore Judah, spent a summer making preliminary surveys to determine whether a route for a railroad over the Sierra was practical. He reported to the "Big Four" in Sacramento that the route by Donner Lake was entirely practical, but at the same time urged that the route up the North Fork of the Feather River should be chosen, for from his data he knew that certainly 1650 feet in altitude would be saved by such selection. That meant that it would save lifting every car that crossed the mountains 1650 feet into the air, and then lowering it down to the level of the great basin between the Sierra and Rocky Mountain ranges.

His was but a hasty, preliminary survey; the careful and expert surveys since made show that the route is not 1650 feet, but 2022 feet lower than the Donner Lake Pass.

For reasons of its own the Central Pacific Company did not accept Judah's advice. Many other railroad builders have since considered the figures but have recoiled before the North Fork Canyon, with its cliffs towering high on both sides and a swift river rolling below.

A Road Built for All Time

But the Western Pacific Company, having full knowledge of the cost of running trains over heavy grades, decided that a road intended to last for all time should be constructed so that it could be operated at the least possible expense and that all possible physical difficulties should be eliminated, and so boldly bearded the lion of that canyon in his den and subdued him.

Those who want to see a mighty triumph of science

and daring over the hostile elements of Nature should pass through that canyon. In the beginning man was given dominion over the world and all its furious moods. The triumph wrought in that canyon makes clear that man has greatly advanced and that nothing will be impossible to mortals when to them the light has fully come.

The eastern terminal of the Western Pacific Railway is Salt Lake City.

The Legend of Salt Lake City

There is a legend, very old, that in the long ago some angels, like some mortals, left their comfortable homes for a summer outing; that they camped one night on the shore of Great Salt Lake. They awoke just when the dawn was flooding the summit of the Wasatch Range with sunbeams, turning the snows to purple and spreading a halo over the valley below; that those visitors took out their pencils and dipping them in the sunbeams, painted the mountains to the east with sombre but immortal dyes; the Oquirrh Range to the west, with gold; gave to the valley below a radiance indescribable and to the lake a deeper blue, then said to each other:

"We will leave our work to be the frame of a picture which man must complete by building here a city fairer than any other city, and around which shall cling an interest such as no other city can command."

Fremont Lingered Here

The ages rolled on, the centuries ebbed and flowed, but only the frame of the picture remained. The savages that roamed the West saw it and praised the Great Spirit for it, old trappers and hunters like Bridger and Carson saw it, the Pathfinder, Fremont, lingered for days under its spell. At last some weary travelers made an encampment in that valley, and a few inspired ones, looking around, said: "Was there ever so marvelous a frame for a picture?"

IN THE WESTERN PACIFIC COUNTRY

Religious Travelers

They were a band of fanatics; they had a religion of their own; they did not care very much for people who professed another religion than theirs, but, borne up by it, they had made the long journey, and as they, toil-worn and sore from the hardships of their journey, and with only the loneliness and the frown of the desert before and around them, they kneeled there on the desert and offered a praise service to their God for His mercies to them.

"What Does it Matter?"

They built some rude homes, they utilized the streams that came down from the hills to soften the soil so that they might cultivate it; when they had enough to eat they were thankful, when they did not they tightened their belts and said: "What does it matter?" So they toiled and prayed and sang, and if there was any repining in their hearts, they smothered it before it found expression on their lips.

The End of the First Generation

So the first generation wore out their lives; but, as the marks of age came, as cheeks grew wrinkled and hands through toil became gnarled, the frown of the desert began to change to smiles, and fruits and marvelous flowers appeared, and, smiling, they said to themselves: "See, our youth has fled, but it is being transferred to the desert and is reappearing with all traces of the earth earthy removed and in the guise of lovely flowers."

The City Beautiful

After a while the loneliness began to pass away. School-houses and churches; the great temple lifted its turrets to the sky; there began to be great commercial houses and elegant homes; one and another railroad found a terminal there; a thrill ran through the hills and they began to pour out their measureless treasures; then the telegraph and a daily press began to sound forth the fact that a great commercial city was growing on the shore of Salt Lake; Progress came and built a capitol there, and if the angels who painted the frame of that city on the mountains near, ages before civilized man knew that there was such a spot, if they, a few years hence, take another outing and camp again on the shore of the inland sea, they will, when they next morning awake and look around, in accord raise the acclaim that the frame has been filled, that the radiant picture is there.

As I was saying, the eastern terminal of the Western Pacific Railway is at Salt Lake.

Then it moves out to the northwest over the route that the Pony Express boys rode, over the route that the tired overland coaches followed.

The River Jordan

As the train nears the great lake it will be in order for passengers to remember that the river they crossed near the city was the Jordan, that the lake at their feet is not only more majestic than the Dead Sea that they read about when they were young and more or less innocent, but that its waters hold in solution $16\tfrac{2}{3}$ per cent salt, which means that if six barrels of it were drawn out and the water evaporated, there would remain one barrel of pure salt, so that had it been there that Lot's wife had "looked back," what she was thereafter would have provoked no curiosity. And if near there they see railroad trains hurrying to and fro and a great structure with low murmurs belching out clouds of smoke, they may know that the trains are bringing copper-bearing ore from a camp twenty miles to the south; that the works reduce 17,000 tons per day and are the greatest copper reducing works in all the world; that the camp which produces that ore has been in operation more than forty years, that the ores at first were gold ores, then changed to silver-lead ores, then, as depth was attained, copper ores with a small percentage of silver and gold were uncovered, and that as mining is now being prosecuted the industry has no rival in majesty and ef-

The Greatest Copper Plant in the World

fectiveness in all this world. The Moving Picture monopoly offered more for an exclusive right to it than it offered for the Panama Canal. The mountains are being literally torn asunder by dynamite and steam dredges; "Jove's Thunder" is obsolete compared with it, and, standing at the base and looking upward, one realizes what Sinai must have been when its summit was wrapped in clouds and darkness and the mountain was shuddering under the foot-falls of the Infinite.

And at night, when the searchlights are ablaze, the dynamite is given full play, the steam shovels are coughing and the trains are roaring, the looker-on says to himself:

"Should perchance my soul take the wrong chute, would Hell itself bring me any surprises?"

The Sea-Gull in Utah

But some of the passengers may be looking at the sea-gulls, wondering at their numbers and how destitute of fear they seem. Such must know that the gull is a sacred bird in Utah, and that a special statute protects them, but the story of them is their far greater protection.

When the "chosen people" were ahungered and were fainting because of lack of food in the desert, the good Book tells us that God caused manna to rain upon them for bread.

The Gulls Save the First Crop

When the first comers to Utah had planted their first crop and depended upon that for the next winter's food, there came a great cloud of locusts, and, as is their wont, they began to destroy every green thing. The people were in despair, for a famine seemed before them. But suddenly the gulls in unknown numbers came, consumed the locusts and saved the crop. They were the manna of the Saints and ever since have been a sacred bird in Utah.

As the train pulls away from the lake and the

white breast of the desert is exposed, the passenger must not ask why such a waste was created, for if, when the train stops at the next station, he will get out and gather up some handfuls of the substance and take it with him to some chemist and have it analyzed, he will learn that its ingredients are almost identical to those out of which Portland cement is manufactured.

Nature's Salt Factory

As the train proceeds the passenger will discover another phase of the desert, and will be told that what he sees is salt, and that if he will go upon it and cut a trench, no matter how long or deep, and will come back in a year, he will find that trench filled with chemically pure salt, for kindly old Nature has some extensive manufacturing plants of her own and is never disturbed by strikes or lockouts, or walking delegates from the industrial workers of the upper world.

The Richness of the Soil

When the trains run through miles of great sagebrush the passengers may learn that the soil under the brush is richer than that in Eastern river bottoms, that all that is needed is water to cause it to produce finer fruits and vegetables and cereals than he ever saw grow in any other country.

The Water Underground

And as all streams in Nevada sink into the ground, in order to find a way to the sea, shrewd men have all over southern Nevada intercepted these subterranean streams by pumps, and now vast tracts are being reclaimed and changed to fruitful fields.

"In the beginning God said: 'Let there be light.'" And to those to whom the full light has come the desert is filled with interest.

Pyramid Lake

When the train reaches a point where, to look southward, the passenger sees Pyramid Lake, it may rest him to be told that if he will strain his eyes to take in the mountains south of the lake, that for

IN THE WESTERN PACIFIC COUNTRY

ten years emigrants with their teams crept slowly along that trail, and almost doubted the wisdom of God for making a waste so desolate, but in that mountain range, only twenty-five miles away, the great Comstock lode lay waiting with its treasures for the coming of men; that since then it has yielded more than one thousand millions of gold and silver; that it was the inspiration which caused the world to cease dreaming of fortunes in thousands and to dream of fortunes in millions.

The Great Comstock Lode

Looking northward he will see where on the road from Susanville to Black Rock, in two years eighty men were slain by savages.

When the train curves into Long Valley the passenger should know that for more than half a century that long narrow valley has been peopled. More than forty years ago the writer of this sketch found in that valley a real philosopher. He lived in a little house down the valley, no other house within seven miles. His name was Marsh and he with his beautiful wife lived there alone. He had a little farm which he cultivated, but it was over a ridge out of sight of the road. He had built his house by the roadside and close beside a great boiling spring, from which ran perhaps eight miners' inches of water. The writer stopped there for a mid-day luncheon. A week before some renegade Piute Indians had murdered a family further down the valley and Marsh had just returned home from an Indian hunt. The few people in the valley had joined together, chased the Indians to cover and killed them, and Marsh had just returned. He had lost his hat, was sun and wind burned black as an Indian, and his clothes, especially the trousers from the knee down, were torn to shreds. The writer asked him what he did in that lonely place to make a living.

Settled for Over Fifty Years

A Wonderful Spring

"Take in washing," was the terse reply.

"How do you manage it?"

"My wife does the washing and," pointing to the spring, "I furnish the hot water."

Sierra Valley — Sierra Valley beyond Beckwith Pass is more a great tableland than a valley. It must contain some five hundred square miles of land and was a chief factor in supplying hay to the innumerable teams that the Comstock so long gave employment to.

Mohawk Valley — Beyond Sierra Valley is Mohawk Valley. It was in Mohawk Valley that old Jim Beckwith lived so long. As the world knows, he was a famous hunter and trapper. About 1852 or 1853 he went into Quincy and told the people that if they would buy supplies enough to last through the winter he and his friend would write up the striking events of his own life, and he was sure that publishers would be glad to publish the manuscript and pay him a royalty which would secure his old age against penury.

Beckwith could neither read nor write, but his friend could. Beckwith was half negro and had a gift of depicting scenes in which he had been a principal in a way which, had he lived, would have made him a leading "progressive."

What They Bought — The money was supplied him and he and his friends "went down below," that is to the Sacramento Valley, to buy supplies. They returned with their purchases in a few days, and when those purchases were examined they were found to consist of some powder and lead, a sack of salt and three barrels of whiskey. "But, Jim, is this all?" was asked him. He replied that it was.

"But did you not need something more?" was next asked him, and he admitted that he would have been glad to get one more barrel of whiskey but was afraid he would "go broke."

IN THE WESTERN PACIFIC COUNTRY

They lived on wild game and whiskey all that winter, but the book was written and it was an interesting book.

Let vegetarians and prohibitionists take notice.

Quincy and Tom Shannon

Quincy was never a mining camp, but was the clearing-house for many surrounding camps in the placer mining days. Spanish Ranch, twelve miles away, was a lively camp for many years. It was there that Tom Shannon lived for ten years, until an appreciative constituency sent him to Congress. He soon made a name there as one of the old-time stalwarts. He was an intimate friend of Roscoe Conkling and would not be reconciled when Grant was defeated in 1880.

Shannon for a long time had the custom-house in San Francisco, and died in that city.

J. Cunningham was the master spirit of Nelson's Point, another mining camp tributary to Quincy. He was the Moses of his precinct, and brought to one a realization of the old feudal days when the peasantry leaned upon the old barons.

To Quincy to Fight a Man

A little out of Quincy lived a miner alone, who about once a week came to Quincy. His name was Sam Smith, about the most perfect man physically that I ever met. One day in Quincy he got into an altercation with a fighter forty pounds heavier than he. When suddenly the fighter, like a stroke of lightning, aimed a terrific blow at his face, with an upper cut Smith struck the fighter's wrist, which sent his aim high in the air, and quietly said: "Try that on your dog or your wife, you are too clumsy to fight a man."

An Incident in Rich Bar

S. O. Brown was the master spirit on Rich Bar in those days. When he came to Quincy he always made a night of it. He came one night and was proceeding to paint the town when he ran upon a notorious loud talker named Snell. They had two or three drinks together, then Snell got noisy and troublesome, and the gentleman from Rich Bar cuffed his ears, knocked off his hat, kicked him out of the saloon and kicked his hat after him. Brown left at daylight for home. About noon Snell made his appearance at the saloon and wanted to know where the fellow was that he was "skylarking" with the night before. After that he was known as "Skylark Snell."

The Crescent Quartz Mill

Billie Bolinger built the Crescent quartz mill at Greenville, on the edge of Indian Valley, and ran it for several years. A brother of General Bidwell of Chico bought a mine near the Bolinger mine, built a mill upon it, worked it several years until finally, from exposure in crossing the mountains in winter, was seized with pneumonia and died at the mine.

A Farming Valley

American Valley was filled with farmers. D. L. Haun had a farm there. He was a brother of Judge Haun who, by appointment, succeeded David Broderick (who was killed by Judge Terry in a duel) in the United States Senate. John Thompson was a farmer and horse raiser. His colt, "Pacific," outfooted plenty of colts that had better records than his. The secret was that Pacific was raised in the lighter air of the mountains, which necessitated bigger lungs than the valley horses needed. When the big lungs were filled with the heavy air of the valley the horse beat his own record by several seconds because of the extra amount of oxygen in his lungs.

A Famous Lawyer

Tom Cox was a famous lawyer there, a thoroughbred that had not been properly bitted and disciplined when a colt. I heard him one day in a Justice's Court address the court, whose jurisdiction has been questioned, as follows:

"Your Honor, yours is not like the District nor the Superior Court. They have stated terms, the commencement of which has to be advertised in advance. You are given much greater discretion. You can open court in the street or the livery stable or the drug store—anywhere. Indeed, your Honor, your court is like a sick oyster, it is always open."

To the Court

An eccentric newspaper man lived there named Lovejoy, a close relative of Owen Lovejoy. I have seen him buy a five-dollar hoop-skirt, put it on over his Prince Albert coat and wear it all day.

Some of the bravest quiet men I ever knew lived there—Yates, Pierce, Byers—indeed that was the rule. R. C. Chambers was a miner who, when I went to Quincy, had been elected sheriff. Later he removed to Utah, opened the Ontario Mine at Parley's Park and from it took more than forty millions of dollars.

Forty Millions from Old Mine

Old Indian George lived there, the kindliest, most cheerful tamed savage in the world. He had a single contest fight with a big cinnamon bear and killed him with a knife, but the bear tore the muscles from one cheek and jaw, one arm and one hip.

A Fight with a Bear

George's wife (Mohala) watched the fight and a few months later became a mother. When that child was two and a half years old its face was a bear's face, and when it walked it was not "the bear that walks like a man," but rather "the man that walked like the bear."

J. B. McGee was perhaps the most prominent miner in Plumas. He was a member of the constitutional convention that formed the first Constitution of California and was many terms in the Legislature.

Member of Constitutional Convention

He went to Nevada and made a large fortune in the Tybo mines. He, with two or three California bankers, bought a great mine in Oregon, made the first payment and built a quartz mill upon it. The second payment came due just as the panic of '93 was sprung; the bankers who were his partners could not help him and he lost all. About eight years ago he obtained another mine on a bond and lease in Oregon, installed a cyanide plant and was beginning to see his way to another fortune when he suddenly died, aged eighty-five. His energy was something that only death could quench.

Sierra Buttes

Due west some twenty miles from Mohawk Valley a trail ran to the Sierra Buttes, a vast low-grade gold deposit which supplied ore to a hundred stamp quartz mill for more than forty years.

Clover, Genesee and Indian Valleys

To reach Clover, Genesee and Indian valleys the traveler from the East turned through a low divide, five miles west of Beckwith Pass. Clover and Genesee valleys forty years ago were occupied mostly by people making butter and cheese for the Comstock mines, though there is copper in the first and gold in the second. Indian Valley is a beautiful valley some 120 miles in area and devoted mostly to farming. From Indian Valley the road enters American Valley from the east, while the more direct road from Mohawk Valley—the road of the Western Pacific—enters the valley from the south.

American Valley

American Valley is a most lovely valley, three miles in diameter and surrounded by magnificent mountains. It was the home of the writer for two years and is a very dear place. Quincy is a typical mountain village, peopled by men and women with whom hospitality is a religion. Fifty years ago it was surrounded by placer mining camps. The miners brought their dust in to sell every Saturday night and Sunday was the liveliest day in the week. It was (and is) the county seat of Plumas County, and many eminent lawyers made their fame there, and all the residents were high-class people.

One summer afternoon a storm swept across the American Valley from the higher mountains to the west. It was just a summer shower, but on its way it was caught by the sunbeams and they built a rainbow from the mountains to the north to the majestic mountains on the south. The points of the arc rested on the hills and the royal arch spanned the whole valley and hung there in splendor for quite ten minutes. There never was such another rainbow. Its colors were all gloriously vivid and distinct.

A Wonderful Rainbow

The ladders up and down which Jacob saw the angels ascending and descending were but commonplace affairs compared with that bridge of purple and of gold.

When emigrants reached American Valley they seldom went any further, at least not the same year. But after 1849 there was a trail over the mountains, and after the first year or two a wagon road, via Spanish Ranch, Magdalen Plains and Berry Creek to Bidwell's Bar, on the Middle or South Fork of the Feather, in the low foothills, and perhaps ten miles east of Oroville. It was a wagon road in summer, a road for pack animals until the snows became too deep and then the mails and an occasional passenger were carried on dog-sleds. Men walked on snow-shoes. It is a delightful journey in the early autumn. The road runs through miles and miles of the great pines of the Sierras. The writer made the journey once on mule back. The first night was spent at Bucks Ranch and during the night six inches of snow fell. The morning was beautiful and the sky had a deep-sea tinge. It was like passing through some vast temple of the immortal gods. All below was white as alabaster. The great trees were columns of that temple. The damp snow clung to the mighty tops of the pines; the sunbeams were playing upon the snow, and looking up one saw a roof of green and white and gold, and the thought that came instantly was: "Why, Solo-

A Stopping Place

A Great Temple

mon's temple no more compared with this than an adobe shanty compares with the Temple of Jupiter of Phidias on the Acropolis of Athens."

Bidwell's Bar

Bidwell's Bar already referred to was a most famous placer mining camp, and the gold taken from it was measured by millions of dollars. Fifty years ago a suspension bridge spanned the river at that point. Around one of its abutments a little plat of green grass was cultivated. Some oranges were left by a teamster there and the seeds of one of them were planted in this plat. The result was a beautiful orange tree. More than forty years ago the tree began to bear fruit and sometimes the strange spectacle was presented of an orange tree standing in fifteen inches of snow with ripe and green oranges on the tree. But stranger still, this ungrafted tree bore fruit so sweet that men sent from all the lower valleys of California for cuttings from this tree, until the navel orange drove all competitors out. A month ago a friend told me that the tree, now grown to lordly proportions, was as vigorous as ever and the fruit was as sweet as of old.

Ripe Oranges with Trees Covered with Snow

The Western Pacific Plunges into North Fork Canyon

It was from American Valley that the Western Pacific road took its plunge into the North Fork Canyon. It had no trail to follow, to build it was a fight against the rocks above and the roaring river below. The eagles from the cliffs above must have looked on astounded as the work went on, but it was accomplished, and more than one of what were called the seven wonders of the world were less wonderful than that triumph. Emerging from the canyon the road again takes to the trail made by the men who found and worked out the mining camps of Cherokee and Yankee Hill, on the Middle Fork of the Feather, which merges with the North Fork a little above Oroville.

IN THE WESTERN PACIFIC COUNTRY

Oroville

There was great mining at Oroville and near Table Mountain, back of Oroville.

An Impossible Request

Harry B. Lathrop had charge of the latter works for a San Francisco company. He went to San Francisco, called upon the directors and informed them that he wanted a fourteen-inch pipe that would bear a vertical pressure of four hundred feet. He was told to call at 10 a. m. the next day, when all the directors would be present. He was on time and found all the directors and the engineer of the company present. Lathrop explained what he wanted, when the engineer, being called upon, declared that the demand could not be complied with, that no pipe that could be made would bear that pressure.

And a Demonstration

On a table near stood a pitcher of ice water and two or three old-fashioned goblets. Lathrop arose and poured one of the goblets full to the brim with water. Then, turning to the engineer, he said: "That does not burst the goblet, does it?"

"Oh, no," was the reply.

"And it would not if the goblet was four hundred feet high if it was strong enough," said Lathrop.

He got the pipe.

Dams on the Feather River

There were several attempts to dam and turn aside the Feather River in the summer when the water was low, to mine the bed of the river, before the coming of the rain in the autumn, but our recollection is that they all failed, though one did succeed at Bidwell's Bar, on the Middle Fork of the Feather. Harry B. Lathrop made a great success in hydraulic mining above Oroville. That was before the "giant" was invented and the pipe had to be controlled by men. A six-inch pipe with a two-inch nozzle under a vertical pressure of three hundred feet is a stormy thing to handle.

The present dredging of the valley below Oroville

is simply to obtain the gold that the boys missed in the long ago before the steam dredge was applied to mining.

Close to the Old Trails

Thus it will be seen that almost every foot of the Western Pacific was built on one or another of the old trails, all except about forty miles down the North Fork Canyon.

The Emigrant The Pony Express The Pullman

At first there was the lonely emigrant, then followed the Pony Express and the stage, then the iron horse. The changes of the years have been many and great. The inner wilderness and desert have been subdued; where all was a wild, many sovereign states have rounded into form, but the impatient traveler on the soft cushions of the Pullman car ought to be impressed with the fact that the foundations of those states have been laid on the hearts of two generations of men and women, who were as brave and true and self-sacrificing a race as ever, in a long fight with hardship and want and sorrow, drove back the frontier, subdued the wilderness, built temples to justice and order and industry and learning and law, and caused the frown of the desert to give way to smiles.

I have followed the Western Pacific to where it debouches into the great valley of California.

Other pens than mine should take up the work there, for the valley has been transformed since I lived there.

A Story About Rats

I think I can make that clear by an incident. When I first went to live in Marysville the rats at night would race over my bed in pairs and in companies. They are sociable chaps when they once get acquainted. After a while the city was inundated by the overflowing Yuba and the backed-up water of the Feather River, and millions of them were drowned. But there were plenty left. When the rains ceased in the spring and under the intense heat the houses became as dry as tinder, a fire broke out one night and swept the city.

Marysville

The previous year a miner, who had made a good many thousands of dollars in placer mining, came down to the city and built a fine block of three-story houses—stores below and offices upstairs. He stood in the street watching the fire. It finally struck his block and in a moment enveloped it in flame, whereupon the ex-miner burst into a great fit of laughter. His friends thought he was crazed by his losses. At last one friend approached and in a sympathetic tone said: "What do you find to laugh about, Jerry?" His reply, choked by laughter, was:

"Is not that fire up there giving those rats h——?"

"The Call of the Wild"

But, after all, those were great old days. All the valley was carpeted with flowers, the air was soft and came to the cheek like a caress, the blue Sierra in the distance seemed ever beckoning the men of the valley to come and seek treasures there; the dawns and sunsets shone down upon the world like the smile of God.

Coaching Days

Speaking of the dawns is a reminder. The California stage company had its headquarters in Marysville and just at dawn the criers began. There were four-horse coaches for the hill country, six-horse coaches for the long valley runs and eight-horse twenty-seven passenger Troy coaches ran between Marysville and Sacramento. The first cry was in a shrill falsetto voice, "Empire Ranch, Rough and Ready, Grass Valley and Nevada." Then followed a heavy bass voice with "Oroville, Chico, Tehama, Red Bluff, Shasta and Yreka." Then a high tenor cried out for Domnville and Camptonville; then like the beating of time, a magnificent baritone voiced its acclaim with "Sacramento, Sacramento," lingering on the final syllable until it rang out on the morning air like the peal of a great bell.

STEEL RAILS ON THE OLD TRAILS

A Forty-eight Pound Melon

There was no fruit in Marysville at that time, but Briggs had a ranch up the Yuba three miles and raised watermelons—and such melons. I remember one that was sent to me that was four feet long and weighed forty-eight pounds.

A Dollar Each for Apples

I remember the first little shipment of Oregon apples that reached Marysville. They retailed at one dollar each. I bought one for a three-year old baby girl that I was in love with—great God, that baby is a great grandmother now.

Mails from the East came once in two weeks.

A Distinguished Citizen

We celebrated the laying of the first Atlantic cable a month after it was laid. We did it partly on account of our fellow townsman, Stephen J. Field, who was so long a Justice of the U. S. Supreme Court. He was a brother of Cyrus W. Field, the father of the cable.

Some Renowned Men

There were stalwart men there, the brightest bar in the State; intellectual chiefs, great men of affairs and industrial kings, William Walker, "the gray-eyed man of destiny," who with his filibusters took Nicaragua and then got himself shot, and plenty more. George Gorham, who for thirty years was secretary of the U. S. Senate, was my near neighbor there. We had lots of politics, too. No one who was not there can get an idea of how hot were the factions. I heard Ned Marshall—he was a know-nothing that year—hold a crowd of thousands from 10 p. m. until 1 a. m., explaining to an enthusiastic audience the sins of omission and commission of the Democratic party. He described the Democratic State Convention held in the Baptist Church in Sacramento in 1854. It was something like this:

Convention in Baptist Church

"The convention being in the house of the Lord I never dreamed of any trouble, and went to hear the proceedings. I waited until the delegates began to draw pistols and bowie knives and then, the room being warm, I went out into the open air. There was a high lumber pile near the church and I sat down behind it. The shady side of it was furthest from the church, so I sat down in the shade.

"Soon a gentleman came by. He was wearing a delegate's badge. He must have thought of some urgent business down town, for he was running. He evidently left the convention in a hurry for he was wearing a window sash around his neck." And Marshall closed in these words:

"Talk of corruption, why the man in the moon held his nose as he passed over Sacramento that night."

We had fine schools, several churches and two daily newspapers. One in every edition for months advocated the building of a plank road out to Empire Ranch, in order to capture the trade of Grass Valley and Nevada City from Sacramento.

It was there that I heard for the first time Col. E. D. Baker speak. The echoes of his voice are in my ears still. I mean the Col. Baker who delivered the eulogy over the body of Broderick, who was killed in a duel with Judge Terry; who, when a Senator of the United States, replied to the speech of Breckinridge and thrilled the Senate; who raised a regiment in Washington and was sent to Balls Bluffs to be sacrificed because he was too near to President Lincoln to suit some others in authority, and who, with his hand in the breast of his coat, went down in an assault by overwhelming numbers.

There were three banks and several assay offices at that time in Marysville. I noticed a quiet man who had worked in one of the assay offices walking the streets several days in succession. I asked him how it was. He told me he had been discharged. I asked how it happened. He replied: "I guess I am too honest," and explained that when a miner

A Window Sash for Collar

Schools and Churches

Col. Baker

Banks and Assay Offices

Gold Dust and Weighing Methods

brought gold dust to the office it was weighed, a receipt given and a time fixed when he should come for his gold bar. That when he had gone the assayer would put from one to ten silver dollars in one scale and as many ounces of dust in the other as would balance the dollars and then make a mistake and empty the dollars back upon the miner's deposit and keep the dust. As gold dust averaged $18 per ounce it will be seen that the assayer did well in his business. The weight of the bar corresponded with the weight of the dust, but the values were shrunk. The assayer assured the miner that there must be some alloy in his dust, silver or platinum or some other metal, and there certainly was when the assayer was through with it.

Amusements

There was lots of fun in Marysville in those days. At first the Chapman family and the San Francisco Minstrels, then Mrs. Waller came and sang, then the stronger ones. Mrs. Chapman, after she had been the mother of eighteen children, supported the great Murdock in the play of "The Stranger." The play went through all right but as soon as it was out Murdock went on a week's drunk.

Matilda Heron came there in her first glory, and she was a glory, sure enough. The Ravelle (French) family and a family of four beautiful Spanish girls from old Spain came and danced.

The Stage in Marysville

Estelle Potter lived in Marysville several years. She with her troupe made a trip north and played one night in Shasta. The play was "The Marble Statues." The company reached Shasta just as night fell. There was no time for rehearsal. So soon as dinner was over the company went to the theatre and the play began. But when Miss Potter reached the point where she had to address, one after another, her ancestors, the first one was a live Chinaman, so was the second, so the whole family. Miss Potter went through the ordeal superbly despite the convulsions of the house, then sought her dressing-room and fell screaming between laughter and hysterics upon a lounge.

The previous morning the manager of the theatre said to his assistant: "What shall we do for statues?" The vagabond replied: "Don't worry, I'll fix that." He had hired Chinamen at $15 each to act as statues, explaining to them that he would be watching in a wing with a gun, and if one of them smiled or moved, he would fill him full of holes. They answered, "All lightie." None of them were killed but it came near killing Miss Potter.

Supplying the Statues

We had other characters in Marysville. One was "Tow-headed Ross." It was believed that he was the leader of a band of robbers, for he always dined finely, rode a magnificent horse and lived expensively, without any apparent business. He would leave the city occasionally and be absent for two or three months, but no one knew where he went. He had flaxen hair and blue eyes, and if he stepped into a saloon and remained a few minutes each man in the saloon was ready to swear that all the time Ross was watching him alone.

"Tow-headed Ross"

He was walking in the outskirts of the town one day and came to where some Mexicans had chickens buried, all except their heads in the ground, and were permitting men to shoot at them at a distance of twenty yards, at "doce pesos"—twenty-five cents—a shot, the winner to have his chicken. Ross asked if he might use his own pistol, and when consent was given he fired six shots in five seconds and won six chickens, while the Mexicans were crying, "Diablo, Diablo."

Some Shooting

There was a real robber band in the foothills east of Marysville, under a famous bandit, Tom Bell.

STEEL RAILS ON THE OLD TRAILS

A Fight

At the time Captain William King was chief of the police of Marysville, he went out after the robbers, came upon them and had a duel with them, he with a revolver, they with rifles.

Next morning a letter came to King, which read as follows:

A Letter

"Chief King: Don't do that any more, for I fear some of my men may forget instructions not to kill a man who is fool enough to fight with a revolver such a company as I have armed with rifles.

Yours truly, Tom Bell."

The Sheriff

Mike Gray was sheriff of Yuba County. To save his own life he was obliged to kill a man. He had no weapon but a four-inch derringer pistol, which he carried in his vest pocket. That night a friend reproached him for going about with no weapon but a derringer. He replied: "I guess you are right, there might be more than one of them next time."

A Dream Realized

One of the sweetest dreams of all the men in California through those years was the possibility of living until the isolation of the State should be removed by the coming of a perfect railroad on the lowest grades, like the Western Pacific, to connect the Golden State with the less favored states of the East.

Sacramento led in giving expression to this hope, through that very greatest of newspapers, the old Sacramento Union.

That journal, in molding public opinion, in furthering every industry and every holy cause, had more power than "an army with banners."

The Great Empire

No State was ever so splendidly peopled as was California. The pick of the world gathered there. As they looked into each other's eyes the thought was, "Never before was an empire like this opened to men. May the brightest and bravest win."

IN THE WESTERN PACIFIC COUNTRY

Now, after three-score years, behold their work,— the transformation in California, of the desert beyond!

What It All Means

The savage subdued; the frontier rolled back; temples everywhere to Industry; to Learning; to Progress; to enlightened Liberty and to Peace.

The splendor of a superb civilization illuminating the land; States rounded into form and answering "Aye" when the roll of States is called; the fields yielding their fruits and flowers; the mountains and the desert their treasures — the history a mighty anthem filled with heroic strophies, with names that will be immortal, with works that will be a wonder when the mighty works of the ancients will be but legends, overshadowed by the achievements of modern men.

The Final Result

And one of these will be the Western Pacific Railway, to build which on easy grades the mountains were stormed in their very fastnesses and compelled through dynamite and gold to surrender a broad and smooth right of way.

FEATHER RIVER ROUTE

GENERAL AND TRAVELING AGENTS

BOSTON, MASS., Percy Van Tassell, Trav. Pass. Agent...728 Old South Building
   J. F. Ryan, Traveling Freight Agent.
BUTTE, MONT., A. B. Ayres, Traveling Passenger Agent......56 East Broadway
CHICAGO, ILL., F. C. Gifford, General Agent............234 South Clark Street
   R. J. Van Dyke, Traveling Passenger Agent.
   F. T. Lonergan, Traveling Freight Agent.
CINCINNATI, OHIO, J. E. Clark, General Agent.........409 Traction Building
   W. H. Bremer, Traveling Freight and Passenger Agent.
   H. S. Roberts, Traveling Freight and Passenger Agent.
CLEVELAND, OHIO, W. E. Zirckel, General Agent......513 Williamson Building
   D. M. Reynolds, Traveling Freight and Passenger Agent.
DETROIT, MICH., O. P. Applegate, General Agent.......1323 Majestic Building
DOYLE, CAL., E. S. Reader, Traveling Freight and Passenger Agent.
ELKO, NEV., F. J. Laben, Traveling Freight and Passenger Agent.
EUREKA, CAL., J. M. Simpson, Freight and Passenger Agent.......210 E Street
FORT WORTH, TEX., J. E. Woodfin, Gen. Agent......405 Cotton Exchange Bldg.
   P. A. Cox, Soliciting Freight Agent.
FRESNO, CAL., T. F. Brosnahan, General Agent...................1035 J Street
   E. C. Preston, Traveling Freight and Passenger Agent.
HONG KONG, CHINA, C. Lacy Goodrich, General Oriental Agent..Kings Building
HONOLULU, T. H., Fred L. Waldron, Ltd., Agents.
KANSAS CITY, MO., E. C. Roxbury, General Agent.........210 Scarritt Arcade
   G. C. Henderson, Traveling Freight and Passenger Agent.
LOS ANGELES, CAL., C. P. Ensign, General Agent.......532 S. Spring Street
   F. R. Kane, Traveling Passenger Agent.
MILWAUKEE, WIS., F. L. Wolfe, General Agent.........816 Majestic Building
   J. C. Connell, Traveling Freight and Passenger Agent.
NEW YORK CITY, N. Y., R. C. Nichol, General Agent............1246 Broadway
   E. Haring, City Ticket Agent.
   R. E. Law, Traveling Freight Agent.
   E. Lovenberg, Traveling Passenger Agent.
OAKLAND, CAL., W. B. Townsend, District Frt. and Pass. Agent..1326 Broadway
   J. H. Chambers, City Passenger Agent.
   A. H. Moffitt, Traveling Passenger Agent.
OGDEN, UTAH. F. Fouts, Agent...................................Reed Hotel
OMAHA, NEB., F. L. Feakins, General Agent.............309 S. Fourteenth Street
   H. G. Bock, Traveling Freight and Passenger Agent.
PITTSBURG, PA., J. T. Neison, General Agent................602 Park Building
   M. F. Walters, Traveling Freight and Passenger Agent.
   J. W. O'Brien, Traveling Passenger Agent.
ST. LOUIS, MO., J. E. Courtney, General Agent.............726 Pierce Building
   J. L. Hohl, Traveling Freight and Passenger Agent.
   J. W. Foley, Traveling Freight and Passenger Agent.
SACRAMENTO, CAL., J. C. Havely, District Frt. and Pass. Agent....729 K Street
   W. C. Dibblee, Assistant District Freight and Passenger Agent.
   J. L. Scott, City Passenger Agent.
   F. E. Lovejoy, Traveling Passenger Agent.
   H. L. Blackstone, Traveling Freight Agent.
SALT LAKE CITY, UTAH, I. A. Benton, General Agent, Pass. Dept..Judge Bldg.
   A. W. Raybould, Passenger Agent.
   R. W. Flandro, Commercial Agent.
SAN FRANCISCO, CAL.........................665 Market Street, Palace Hotel
   J. G. Lowe, District Passenger Agent.
   R. V. Crowder, City Ticket Agent.
   W. H. Davenport, General Agent, Freight Dept.
   H. C. Brown, Traveling Freight Agent.
SAN JOSE, CAL., J. Q. Patton, General Agent..........42 E. Santa Clara Street
   D. S. McCrone, Traveling Freight and Passenger Agent.
STOCKTON, CAL., H. T. Holmes, Traveling Passenger Agent.
   J. H. Mettler, Traveling Freight Agent.
YOKOHAMA, JAPAN, C. Lacy Goodrich, Gen. Oriental Agent....17 Water Street

Printed by Libri Plureos GmbH in Hamburg,
Germany